Cover design: made by the author using Canva
Illustrations: made by the following artists on Canva:
pixabay, Nadiinko, Victoria rusyn, graphix's images,
vintage illustrations, One Line, By Rikaru, jirwan73

For more information, zazzera.arts@gmail.com

ISBN 978-82-693546-0-7 (Hardcover)
ISBN 978-82-693546-1-4 (Paperback)

Second edition
Susanne Zazzera

About the author

Susanne Zazzera works as a biologist in Norway. She finds much of her inspiration in the natural world, which is clear in her first publication *The Metamorphosis of You*. She started writing in order to heal after heartbreak and regularly posts her poems on Tiktok under @for_the_healing. In her spare time, she also enjoys painting and going for walks in nature.

Foreword

Like so many before me, I have experienced how incredibly painful heartbreak can be. The only thing that seemed to ease the pain was reading poetry. It made me understand that my feelings were valid and that I was not alone in my situation.

As a coping mechanism, I also started to write. Some of the poems in this book originate from my first heartbreak, which happened over five years ago. Over the years (and after many heartbreaks, big and small) I was eventually left with this collection that you are about to read.

I hope you find comfort in my words.

Susanne Zazzera

The Metamorphosis of You

Table of contents

The Metamorphosis of You

the butterfly goes through
four stages in its life
and it is only during the last one
that it gains the ability to fly

maybe
just maybe
this is how it works
for us humans too

Phase 1 - the egg

falling in love

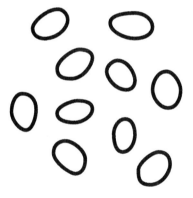

I knew I had fallen for you
when my thoughts automatically
drifted to you for comfort
you were the first thing on my mind
after waking up
and the last thing I saw
before falling asleep at night
you followed me everywhere I went
there was no escaping my feelings
anymore

The Metamorphosis of You

I catch myself dreaming of you
when I close my eyes
my head on your chest
our fingers intertwined
your soothing voice assuring me
there is nowhere else
you would rather be
and in this fleeting moment
time stands still
and everything is just
right

the feeling of warm water
embracing your skin in a bath
the softness of freshly washed sheets
when drifting off to sleep
the sound of birds singing melodies
outside your bedroom window
the sight of the sun rising
leaving the sky painted with colors
the tightness of a hug from a loved one
you haven't seen in a while

these are the sensations I long for
but none of them come close
to the feeling of
your hand stroking me
your gaze catching mine
your voice softly speaking
none of them come close
to you

she asked me
what is your perception of love
and immediately
I told her about you

because to me
you are the embodiment of it
you wear love so gracefully
it flows through you so effortlessly
emanates from your very being
and turns everything you touch
into gold

when you look at me,
the butterflies in my stomach
twirl in anticipation

after being on my own for so long,
I forgot how someone
can make you feel so small

looking for their approval
in everything you do,
desperately wanting them
to notice your efforts,
smiling every time their name
lights up your screen

fearfully hoping
that this time
everything will be different

in my next life,
I hope to be a butterfly
that way
I can always be with you

land on your shoulder
when you need companionship
and show you the way when you
seek guidance

I never planned on catching these feelings
but now I am drowning
desperate for your love
and I hate the sensation of needing you
because I had just learned
that I am enough on my own
until my eyes meet yours
and suddenly
I am *not* anymore

tell me
if we were not made
to love each other
how come your palm
holds my face so perfectly
how come my head
rests so naturally
on top of your shoulders
how come our fingers
wrap around each other
like parts of a puzzle finally
coming together

I found myself in a place
where simply holding hands with him
felt scarier and more intimidating
than spending the night
with any other man
I felt more naked and vulnerable
just from his eyes meeting mine
than I had ever before
by any man undressing me

to me,
love is not some grand gesture
it is not planning a surprise vacation
or picking out an expensive ring

It can be, but mostly love is
bursting out in laughter
because your partner makes a funny face
it is sharing a slice of cake
because there was only one left
it is sensing when they need space
and when they need a shoulder to cry on
it is even admiring
how soft and sweet they look
as they drift off to sleep

it is the small things
the subtle things
that shows just how much love
you have for each other

The Metamorphosis of You

I am afraid to lose myself in you
to lose the person I have grown into
these past years
independent and confident

I am afraid I will put my life on hold
turn down opportunities
drift away from my friends
because I have done so before
stopped focusing on myself
for the sake of someone else

I think we both knew
it wasn't destined to last
yet it felt so good
to be held in your arms
touched by your hands
kissed by your lips

I had never felt such warmth
from any man before
it scared me just how much
I wanted you to stay

Phase 2 - the caterpillar

breaking

I wonder who came up
with the word "heartbreak"
because to me, it feels more
like my whole being is breaking
every fiber of my body
every inch of my soul
fighting to endure the pain

like an egg cracked open
I am now left entirely naked
and vulnerable
forced to protect myself
from the outside world
the people who hurt me
and from me
blaming myself

the recipe for heartbreak:

a soft heart
one gentle soul
two cups of trust
a pinch of hope

I did not expect
how capable I would be
of loving you
or how incapable you would be
of loving me

The Metamorphosis of You

- fragile
- caution
- handle with care
that is what the label
for my heart
should say

please love me gently

there are days
when I want to scream to you
just how much you hurt me
express my feelings of rage
and betrayal

then there are days
when all I want
is rewind to the moments
of resting on your chest
you peacefully kissing
my forehead

it confuses me,
just how much I hate you
and just how much I love you
all at the same time

you must have known how
deeply I had fallen for you
when I held you in my arms
when I looked at you in awe
and kissed you good night
you must have known
when I told you
I loved you

maybe you knew
but chose to ignore
or maybe you didn't believe
that anyone was capable
of loving you
the way that I did

truthfully,
I don't know which is worse

I am very much
a "suffer in silence" type of person
but the suffering that followed you
was anything but silent

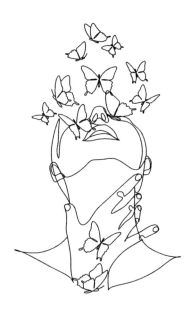

why did you invite me in
when you had no intention
of letting me stay

why did you touch my heart
if you didn't care
about making it bleed

the worst part was
knowing it had to end
but not being strong enough
to end it

being unhappy
yet still thinking
the alternative
would somehow be worse

you were like a burning house
and even with the damage
I still called you home
I sat and watched as the walls fell apart
because even though they were breaking
I had nowhere else to go

it was so confusing to me
that the same hands
that embraced me with love
for so long
were the same hands
that would eventually break me
how could the person
who patched me up
also be the one who stabbed me?

isn't it ironic
that when you were gasping for air
because you felt trapped by my presence
I was gasping for air
because without you
I could not even breathe

there is not enough space
to fill the void in my heart
not enough hands
to feed my hunger for touch
not enough time
to end my longing for your love

you were so blinded
by the way they hurt you
I think you forgot to see
just how much you were hurting me
in the process

your name
has carved itself onto my skin
like a tattoo I am starting to regret
but can't yet afford to have removed
a permanent reminder
of the damage you caused

The Metamorphosis of You

I remember when we ended it,
he told me I deserved someone better

I wondered for how long
he had held that belief
how long he had known
I should have been treated better
yet was not willing to treat me
the way he said I deserved

I wondered how long
he had neglected my needs
all the while knowing I had them
all the while knowing
they could be met

I wondered how long
he had known there would be
someone else out there
ready to give me all that he didn't
but still, not willing to let me go

how was I supposed to know
that love was not meant
to feel like that
when all I had ever known were
the small crumbs of affection
you spared me

I am done
giving my heart to people
who are undeserving of my love

I am sick
of fighting for affection from men
who see me as disposable

I am tired
of draining myself for lovers
who have no intention
of loving me at all

my thighs were not made
to satiate your hunger
my hips not created
to feed your starvation
my lips not formed
to satisfy your needs

I was made
to erupt volcanos
to move whole mountains
to break the waves
of the ocean

I was whole
long before your eyes
lingered on my chest

if only for a day:

if only for a day
I want to feel like
I am not just an option
not just a familiar face
a convenient distraction
someone to text at 2 a.m.
when everyone else is asleep
if only for a day
I want to feel like I don't have
an expiration date
in their life

forgive me
for confusing your lust
with love

forgive me
for believing
you wanted my soul
when you were simply aching
for my body

I wanted you to hold me
and tell me it would all be alright

but then I remembered,
you were the reason I was not
and no amount of comfort from you
could ever make me feel alright again

there once was a girl
so pure even the water envied her
her soul was soft and gentle
and like a flower, she bloomed
more beautiful each day

but the thing about flowers is
people pick them
place them in their homes
claim them as "theirs"
as if they can possess something
that was never meant to be owned
as if they can tame something
that was always meant to be wild

but then one day,
they forget to give it water
the leaves begin to crumble
petals start to fall
so, they toss it away
and eventually,
replace it with someone new

I tightened my grip
because I wanted you to stay
but as my fingers closed in
you slipped away

when you left,
you took a piece of me
with you
I have been searching for
that piece ever since

in drunken nights
and short-lived distractions,
but no empty bottle
or passionate kiss
has ever come close
to the feelings
you used to stir in me

still, I continue the search
in hope that something or someone
may one day come close

The Metamorphosis of You

was it always your intention to leave
once you got what you wanted?
or did you change your mind
along the way?

these are the questions
your silence left me
and your silence is so loud
I can't hear anything else

is it too much to ask
for someone who recognizes
that there is more to me
beyond my body

that I have qualities
that make me capable of
achieving remarkable
things

Is it too much to ask
for someone who does not
take me for granted
but appreciates me
for all that I am

someone who is excited to
love me and all that
I ever will be

I have this habit
of confusing lust with love
every time someone new finds
their way into my life,
I foolishly believe
we have the same admiration
for each other in our eyes

I have no fear
that they may look at me differently
from how I look at them
I have no doubt in my mind
that the words they tell me
will hold true now until the end

there is not even an ounce of insecurity
when they treat me in a way
many may label "too good to be true"
because in my heart I know I deserve no less
than what the best man can do

even after being deceived by men who
never had my best interest at heart,
it is still a foreign concept to me:
craving someone's body
but pretending to want a soul full of art

I don't know how many of these
I have left in me

how many times can I lift myself up
after being disappointed again
how many times can I start over
after another person leaves

asking the same questions
to different faces
hoping for new answers

I started to realize
it was never about
what I felt for you

it was about
how I felt about myself
in your presence
safe, wanted, loved

those were the feelings
I started craving when you left
and it didn't matter anymore
that you weren't the one
giving them to me

I told him I missed him
but the truth was
I only told him
because I wanted him to say it back

it wasn't him that I missed
I missed having someone miss me

Phase 3 - the chrysalis

healing

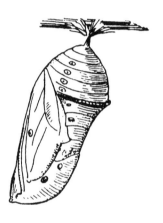

I weaved a cocoon around me
tucked myself in
and sat in my solitude
de-centered men from my life
detached myself from my past
let go of relationships
and then finally, I was ready
to start healing

The Metamorphosis of You

it is not talked about enough
the need for rest and isolation,
the need for healing and restoration,
the need for processing and reflection

instead of always jumping
from person to person
bringing past problems
to new situations

the cycle will continue
until you make a home within
yourself and when it is time
emerge from the chrysalis

but until then,
give yourself the love
you so desperately seek
from everyone else

I thought you broke my heart
when you left,
but the truth is:
I broke my own heart by staying

when you walked away,
I could finally return home
to myself again

I am loved
by the people around me
for my empathy and ambition

I am loved
by the moon and her stars
for recognizing their beauty

I am loved
by the butterflies in my garden
for providing them with sweet nectar

but most importantly
I am loved by myself
for taking care of my heart
cultivating my crafts
tending to my soul

I am loved,
and that is enough,
even if it is not by you

I had so much love to give
when you said you didn't want it
I was not sure what to do

but then, a voice told me
"give it to the one who needs it the most"
so I gave it to myself

I don't know why
we pride ourselves
in not caring for each other
as if it is something to be proud of
to have a closed-off heart
as if it is desirable
to be unable to feel

it takes courage
to realize someone you love
is also breaking you
and therefore, letting them go

removing them from your life
when every limb in your body
aches to be by their side again

like an addict craving drugs,
you long for their presence,
yet fully aware
that the euphoria they give you
will only last for hours
and that the excruciating pain that follows
will never be worth the high

I thought losing you
would mean the end
to my happiness

ironically,
I can't remember a time
being more content than now

The Metamorphosis of You

"where does the love go," you ask,
when the person you used to gift it to
no longer wants it
well, let me tell you, darling

it goes towards the gentle people around you
to the sight of sunsets and rainbows
the smell of flowers and herbs
the sound of music and laughter
the feeling of the sun on your face
to all the beautiful things in life

but most importantly,
it goes towards yourself

the flowers will bloom again,
and so will you
the stars will shine again,
and so will you
the sun will rise again,
and so will you
the butterflies will fly again,
and so will you

when you have been disappointed
so many times
because your heart has shattered
again and again
and the parts no longer seem to fit
after desperately trying
to piece them back together
you start feeling numb,
careless, indifferent,
no longer able to feel the pain

and although it might protect
your fragile heart from breaking,
it will also stop it from loving

you cannot feel the warmth of love
without the risk of getting hurt
you see, they come in pairs
so, to accept love
is to accept the risk
of reliving the pain all over again

I used to hate you
for the pain you made me feel
now, I hate even more
that the heartache you inflicted
numbed my ability
to feel anything at all

What pains me is knowing that the people who hurt me continue to do so. Not by intention, but by the scars they left. They live their lives happily unaware of how their actions and the words they spoke still affect me, as if their lack of effort somehow reflected my worth. Even after years of healing, they hold power over me. Still, their ghosts imply that I am unworthy of *love*.

while healing from heartbreak,
you are grieving the loss of a person
who is still among the living

you may feel bad for hurting so much
when they are still alive and well,
but even though they didn't die,
their love for you did,
and they decided that walking
this Earth without you
was better than having you by their side

so please, be easy on yourself
when you try to belittle your pain

beware the men
who give you compliments
only when they want something
in return

beware the men
who are generous
only when they get their will

beware the men
who tell you they love you
only when your feet
are placed on top of their shoulders

a gentle reminder:

you deserve more
than late-night texts,
visits in the dark,
questionable intentions,
and empty promises

if you intend to love me
only in halves,
it is better you don't love me
at all

The Metamorphosis of You

I have spent many restless nights
cursing your name
wondering how you
broke me so easily

eventually, I realized,
although you were in the wrong,
I was not the helpless victim I had
convinced myself I was
I chose to stay
when I knew I should have left
and *that* was my mistake

after a while
the anger started to fade
I began to realize
that although I didn't deserve it
I still had responsibility
for accepting too much
and expecting too little
from you

I tell them I'm fine,
and for the most part I am,
but then some days,
I fall to the floor,
unable to speak

all I can think about
is how badly you hurt me,
or perhaps even worse,
how I let you

When he left, I thought there would be no more love in my life. But love can be so much more than just romantic. It was in those moments I felt the most loved by everyone else. Through small acts of kindness. Empathic words and understanding looks from people I barely knew. People stretched out their hands, lent me their ears, showed me that life was indeed not devoid of love at all.

my heart is not a home
for temporary people
my body, not a refuge
for lost souls
searching for salvation

what do you do
when you crave intimacy
but at the same time
fear getting too close to someone

what do you do
when you don't want to be alone
but also don't want to depend
on anyone ever again

what do you do
when you desire love
but the very thought of it
also makes you shiver

what do you do
when the thing
you want the most
is also your biggest fear

The Metamorphosis of You

they never tell you
about the aftermath
of a broken heart
they never tell you
there will be difficulties
beyond getting over
the person who hurt you

that you will have fears
about falling in love again
or that will hold yourself back
because the memory of the pain
has carved itself into your skin
and even the slightest touch
is enough for you
to start pulling back

forgive me
if I cannot give you everything at once
for I have been hurt one too many times
to pour myself into people
not capable of handling my heart

be patient with me
and you will see
just how much love
I have to offer

the hardest part of healing a broken heart
is not getting over the person who hurt you,
it is learning how to trust again

forgiving past lovers is difficult
but not doubting the words and actions
of new ones feels impossible

breaking down the walls
that once protected you so fiercely
when doing so puts your heart at risk

being vulnerable with someone
when your entire body wants to resist
because there is always a chance
it might end badly again
that is the hard part

if you want to leave,
please leave now

please leave now,
before I tell my mom how your fingers
fit so perfectly inside my hand

please leave now,
before I let my friends know that the color
of your eyes suddenly became my favorite

please leave now,
before my mind dares to imagine
how perfect we could be together

please leave now,
before my heart becomes so full of you
I can barely call it my own

please leave now,
for if you do so later,
I'm not sure how
I will be able to cope

The Metamorphosis of You

at first
I wanted you to promise me
you would never leave
I wanted you to assure me
that we were supposed
to stay together forever
that you would never grow
tired of loving me
even with a face full of
wrinkles and my hair turning grey

but then I realized,
love does not work like that,
it cannot be forced or coerced
and if it is,
that is not love

we praise flowers for their beauty
forgetting that even the least pretty flower
still provides leaves for hungry caterpillars
and nectar to starving butterflies

seek a love that doesn't chain you
but instead sets you free
a love that doesn't blind you
but makes everything look clear

I hate that I feel like
I have to water myself down
in fear of being too much

I hate that I feel like
I have to pretend
to not care as much as I do
or let you wait before I can reply
so I don't come off
as too interested

as if that is not the point of all this:
to find someone
you don't need to hold back with,
someone who loves
that you have so much to give

The Metamorphosis of You

there will be days when your pain
makes it impossible for you
to leave your bed
when your only mission
is just to survive

then, there will be days when you laugh
and shake your head in disbelief
because you can't understand
why you even used to like them

still after that, there will be days
when you are reminded of the pain
and it will be too much to handle
so you will fall to the floor once again

this time, you'll feel guilty
because you thought that by now
you would be healed,
but please remember,

healing does not happen in a straight line
nobody can tell you
how you are supposed to feel
not even the voice in your own head

if he wants to go,
let him

hold the door open
and say your goodbyes
wish him only the best
even if that was not what he gave you

but don't keep the door open
he was not for you
and that is OK
do not let him fool you
into thinking he might be one day

he showed you his true form
believe him now
or you will regret it later

piece by piece,
I shed the layers,
hoping that one day
I might get to the core
of who I am
without him

the first week will hold more pain
than you have ever encountered
you will try to keep your mind busy all day
only to be haunted by their ghost at night

after a while,
the breakdowns will hit less often
until one day, they will happen so rarely
you'll almost forget you had them

eventually, you'll start to forget about
the person you once thought you
could never live without
but even with them gone,
their ghost will still affect you

now, you must learn
how to trust again
how to love again
and it will be the most terrifying thing
you've ever had to do

Phase 4 - the butterfly

ascending

The Metamorphosis of You

as she grows,
the snake sheds her skin
to make room for the new version of herself
like her, you must also learn to say goodbye
to the old version of you

peel them off your skin
let them go,
they serve only as a reminder
of the past, look back to see how far you
have come, but do not try to shrink
yourself to fit your old form again
it will only be painful
like wearing old clothes
that have become far too tight

at some point,
you cannot grow any further
then, it is time
for a full transformation

this is the time you mold yourself
into something else entirely
this is the time you evolve so much
your old way of living becomes unrecognizable
the way you used to view the world
becomes nothing but a distant memory
the way you used to wish for
and entertain certain situations
will feel strange

now, everything you do is rooted in love
love for yourself
and love for the people who hurt you
because you know they served a purpose
in your life
so, you thank them for the lessons
and you let them go

New Year's Resolution:

in the upcoming year,
my goal is to allow myself to love
to love without judgment
to love without fear

and equally as important,
to let myself be loved
because I am deserving of it
I trust myself to be strong enough
to walk away from any situation
where my needs are not met

I promise to create boundaries
to speak my truth
even if it hurts, even if it means
I have to let people go
because I deserve a love
without indifference

I am ready to heal
to grow
to love

this is the year
I don't allow anyone to use me
to silence me
or put out my fire
this is the year I shine so bright
some may have to clench their eyes
but they will also be grateful for the
warmth of my fire

to the people I hurt,

I am sorry
I was not conscious enough
to recognize I was hurting you
I am sorry I could not see
the ways my behavior impacted you
I am sorry I was too preoccupied
with protecting myself
that I forgot to protect you from me

I know now
that what I did was wrong
I used my own pain to neglect yours

they say hurt people hurt people
today, I break the cycle
today, I refuse to continue
to give my pain to others
instead, I will mend it from within

I hope you heal from
the trauma I caused

The Metamorphosis of You

I will no longer be the chill girl

the girl who puts up with your bullshit
just to keep you around
the girl who accepts way less than she deserves
so she isn't left alone

I will call you out
when you cancel our plans last minute
when you show up too late
leaving me wondering where you've been

I will let you know
when you are not giving me enough
because I deserve someone who will

when a child falls from a tree
she may grow up to believe
that all trees are dangerous
she might even refuse
to ever climb again

the same can happen
when we experience heartbreak
the memory of the pain
stops us from trying again
because we are afraid
of what might happen if we fall

but it is only as you fall
that you get the knowledge
of which trees
are safe enough to climb

they tell you you're soft and sensitive
as if it's an insult
as if feeling all the emotions of the world is bad
but I would rather feel everything all at once
than feel nothing at all

I used to think
I would love you forever
that even after years apart
my heart would still have a piece of you in it
even after finding someone else
you would still be on my mind
at night

but here I am
you haven't crossed my mind
in a very long time
and when you sometimes do
I don't long for our past
but appreciate how far I have come
sine you

a letter to past lovers

I don't know if you will ever read this,
but if you happen to stumble upon it
at some point in your life
I want you to know
that I have forgiven you

it took all of me to get over you,
and it took even more to find the courage
to trust enough to love again
still, things come up for me at times
when I am reminded of your actions
and the words you spoke

you probably weren't aware
that some of the things you did
would haunt me for years to come
if only in small and subtle ways
now I know they were only
a reflection of you
and had nothing to do with me

I hope you heal too,
so the next person won't have to

I don't know why
I fall so hard, so fast
I don't know why
I get so broken when they leave
I don't know why
I feel everything so deeply
as if the universe took the emotions
from a whole city
and poured them all into me

maybe it's because
I am strong enough to hold them
or maybe everyone else dimmed their feelings
in order to survive
and then forgot to turn them back on

you deserve a healthy love

a stable love
a gentle love
a grounding love
a comforting love
a healing love
a calming love
an abundant love

I hope you find it

I paused for a moment
and I thought about the way I loved them
and suddenly, I realized *I* was proof
my very existence was proof that
the love I sought existed
that it was possible to find unconditional love
because I myself loved unconditionally

she learned to live without you
she learned to love herself again
to enjoy moments alone
to not look for you
in every room she entered
or every pair of eyes that met hers
to be content with knowing
it could not have happened
in any other way

I think the biggest lesson
was learning
I didn't need anyone else
that I was OK on my own
and even though
some days were lonely
the majority are not

I no longer worry
if something I do or say
might drive anyone away
I no longer worry
that someone will not meet
the expectations I have for them

I am free
not because I can do what I want
but because their lack of effort
is no longer weighing me down
because I can be myself fully
and no man will ever be able
to take that away from me again

when we demand an apology
from the people who broke us
in order to move on
we give them power

we want them to explain their actions
what they were thinking
or how they could be so cruel
but the reasons they have
will not make a difference
the only closure we need
is knowing they knew it was wrong
but chose to do it regardless

there will come a point,
after you've had enough time to process,
you'll realize just how much you put up with
it will make you pull your hair in frustration
you'll wish you could go back in time
just to scream to your past self
to leave that person or situation

but you only did what you thought was right
with the awareness you had at the time
you must understand
you can't blame the butterfly
for not being able to fly
before it had time to develop its wings

plant a seed and observe it for some time
it may appear not to have grown at all,
but trust me when I say,
some progress is not always seen

because belowground,
the roots are establishing
collecting and storing nourishment
to make sure the plant has
everything it needs
before it can make its big leap
toward the light

"but what if it ends badly," she asked

oh darling, but what if it doesn't?
what if, for the first time, you
actually end up flying?

you have been waiting for a while now
for that special person

for someone who yearns to touch your soul
instead of your body
someone who undresses you
not with their hands
but with their gaze
someone who gives you warmth
not from their skin
but from their gentle heart

I know sometimes it feels like
"the one" will never come
because the world is full of people
who wouldn't hesitate to spend the night with you
only to leave as soon as the sun rises
but sharing your company with them
will only make you feel even more lonely
and having them fill your time
will only make you feel even more empty

I know it may be difficult,
but I promise you this:
every time you reject the people
who are not meant for you
you grow closer to finding the person who is

Up until now, I had thought of myself as a victim. I was confused as to why I was always so unlucky with love. I told myself I didn't deserve to be treated so badly. I gave them so much, yet all they did was take what they could without ever offering anything in return. Although I didn't see it at the time, I was the very person holding me back. I allowed people like that into my life because I had become so certain that no good men existed. I settled for the unworthy because I thought it was better than being alone. I didn't realize I had a choice. I didn't realize that even being alone, all alone, was better than ever allowing them to stay in my life. And I didn't realize healthy love was actually an option.

You see, it was never about meeting the right person, it was about opening myself up to the idea that the right person was out there. And that even if I didn't find them, I would still be *OK* on my own.

at first, it scared me
falling for you and losing control
suddenly
I had so much love and when
you have so much love
you also risk losing it
it can be taken from you
at any second
by a stranger driving at night
by an untreatable disease
or even by the very person
giving it to you

you can never be certain of how
long it will last
but not knowing when it will end
is far better
than not having it at all

The Metamorphosis of You

will you love me
when my flowers start to rot
when my lakes turn to ice
and my roots begin to freeze

will you love me
when I'm cold
when my hands begin to shake
and my voice start to tremble

will you love me
in the winter
when nights grow long
and the sun is rarely seen

will you love me
even when I struggle to see
that spring is just around
the corner

you   know,
all my life,   I was taught
love was supposed to be hard
It wasn't until I met you
I realized just how
soft it actually
could
be

The Metamorphosis of You

when you asked me
what I was looking for
I gave you a vague answer
because I didn't want to scare you
how could I tell you
when you were still just a stranger
that I was looking for someone who
would go to the ends of the world with me
someone who would not hesitate
to choose me in this lifetime
and for in all to come

I was so startled when you told me
you were looking for "the one",
that you were far too old to be playing games
because I was so used to men
with the intention of doing just that
it took me by surprise
the level of maturity and bravery you had
you were not afraid to speak your truth
even before you knew it was
my truth as well

thank you for loving the parts of me
I deemed unlovable because
of past relationships

thank you for being patient with me
when I needed time to trust you

thank you for never pushing me
or making me feel guilty
for not giving you everything all at once

thank you for giving me the space
to grow on my own

thank you for letting me be sensitive
and emotional with you

thank you for reassuring me
and not making me question
how you feel about me

thank you for doing everything
the others never would

and all of a sudden,
there it was:

the mature and healing love
I had been searching for all this time
and for the first time
I could see so clearly why it
was never meant to be
with any of the others

sometimes, I forget
I am safe with you
that I don't have to question
your intentions
or your feelings toward me

sometimes, I forget
that I can bring up our future
without fearing it might scare you away
that what I say will be heard
and you will listen
because you want to learn
how to love me better

sometimes, I forget
because with the others
I was always on edge
prepared for them to tell me
things I didn't want to hear
that I was only a stop along the way but
would never be
the final destination

for the first time, I felt safe
because, even if your love for me fades,
the love I have for myself never will
the choices I make
will no longer be out of fear of losing them
but to keep me from losing myself

it frightens me
how close I was to never meeting you
because a piece of me
had given up on finding love
for a while, I didn't even think it was possible
to find someone so kind and beautiful
I thought men like you
only existed in fairytales

but still
here we are,
living our happily ever after

even before I knew you existed
I was looking for you
in everyone else

time after time
I was disappointed
because they didn't have
your witty sense of humor
or your kindhearted spirit
some had many of your good qualities
but they were always accompanied
by others that were not

that was until I found you
the one my soul recognized
as having everything I was looking for
and then even some more

with our souls intertwined,
I surrendered in your arms
and I knew I was safe
because your eyes spoke of softness
and your hands, of warm embrace

The Metamorphosis of You

our love is eternal
it will burn longer than the sun
grow taller than the trees
and thicker than the forest
it will watch the leaves turn orange
and then see the greening once again
over and over
whole eons will pass
but our love will only grow
stronger

it took me so long to realize
that love is not supposed to be
a rollercoaster of highs and lows
never knowing which version
of your partner you get today

love should be calm, and easy
forming naturally
like a soft breeze
instead of a hurricane
flowing, like a river
not a constant shift
between damaging floods
and terrible draughts

the recipe for ~~heartbreak~~ love:

a soft heart
one gentle soul
two cups of trust
a pinch of hope

The Metamorphosis of You

dear butterfly,

you completed all the stages
that many before you could not
you transformed
into someone stronger, wiser, braver
now, you can spread your wings

your wounds have become scars
and with time they shall fade
but the scars will never fully vanish
you carry them with you
wherever you go

they remind you of what you survived
and are not a sign of weakness
but that of strength and courage
so take great pride in

the metamorphosis of you

because despite it all

here you are

ready to fly

a final note:

the phases of metamorphosis may confuse you into thinking healing is linear. That once you are over the person who broke you, you have fully formed your wings and are ready to find another transformed soul. But you may still need more time and more people might hurt you before you are ready to fly. It might take months, it might take years. In the mean time just know, that this book will be here to comfort you again.

Acknowledgments

First, I want to thank my friends and my family for buying me ice cream and lending me their shoulders. For giving me advice and sharing their wisdom, even when I didn't want to listen. For being there for me when I needed them most.

I also want to thank the people who follow me or have read my poems on TikTok (@for_the_healing). You have encouraged me to keep sharing my words and made me realize how many people experience the same feelings I do.

Next, I want to thank my exes and failed situationships. Even though they hurt like hell, without them, this book would not exist. And of course, I want to thank my dear partner Alihussein, who inspired many of these poems. The very catalyst of my own metamorphosis and the one who made it all worth it in the end.

Last, I also want to thank *you,* the very person holding this book. Whether you bought it on your own or because your friend forced you to as a "you'll feel less alone" kind of gift, thank you.

Enjoyed this book?

Please consider leaving a review on Amazon or Goodreads. Reviews and ratings help me to reach more people as an indie author!

Thank you.

Printed in Great Britain
by Amazon